cartoon MAGIC

N

NORTH LIGHT BOOKS
CINCINNATI, OH

Visit our Web site at www.artistsnetwork.com for information on more resources for artists.

04 03 02 01 00   5 4 3 2 1

A catalog record for this book is available from the U.S. Library of Congress.

ISBN 1-58180-229-3

American Editor: Diane Ridley Schmitz
Editorial Production Manager: Kathi Howard
Production Supervisor: Sara Dumford
American Designer/Production: Kevin Martin
Studio Manager: Ruth Preston

Contents

Part 1: Drawing People, Animals, Aliens and Stuff!

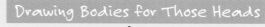

CRASH!

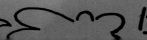

Part 1

Part People, Animals, Objects and Aliens

Cartoon artschool

Welcome to Cartoon artschool. Here's all you need to get started!

CARTOON KIT

Before you begin, you'll need a cartoon-making kit. These four items are essential:

2B PENCIL
This is a soft pencil, great for drawing and easy to erase.

ERASER
PAPER
Any plain white paper with a smooth surface.

A WINDOW...
Yes, a window! See Window Lightbox below.

YUMMY!

2B'S THE BEST!

ALSO HANDY...
FELT-TIP PENS
WATERCOLORS
BRUSHES
CRAYONS & COLORED PENCILS

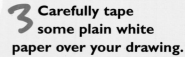

WINDOW LIGHTBOX

Professional cartoonists use a lightbox – a lightbulb in a box that shines light through drawings, so they can trace over them. You can use a window and some masking tape instead. Here's how...

1 Copy a basic cartoon face on to a piece of plain paper.

2 Now, make sure your window is firmly shut. Fix the paper to the window with masking tape, so you don't leave any marks on the glass.

3 Carefully tape some plain white paper over your drawing.

4 Your original cartoon will show through, so now you can trace the outline and add eyes, a funny nose, hair, teeth – anything! Look at the next pages for ideas.

HERE'S HOW!

Now try thissss

Drawing a cartoon head is really easy! Start with a circle - it doesn't have to be perfect - and you're ready to go...

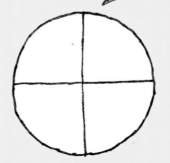

1 Using a 2B pencil, divide the circle into four. Don't press too hard, as you'll erase these lines later.

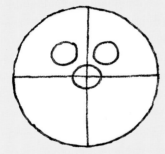

2 For the nose and eyes, draw a circle where the lines cross, and two above, on either side of the line.

3 A dot in each eye makes a pupil, and a line makes the mouth. Now you have a basic cartoon face.

SMILING For a smiling face, follow steps 1 and 2. Add the pupils and draw a curved line for the mouth. Curved lines above the eyes make eyebrows.

SAD Two lines for eyebrows, and a downward-curving mouth make a sad face. Draw each ear so that the top of the ears are level with the bottom of the eyes.

MOODY FACES

ANGRY
Use slanting eyebrows, and a lopsided curve for the mouth.

SICK
Ugh! He's eaten too many sweets... Look at those bulging cheeks.

WORRIED
Uh-oh, he's in trouble...

Cartoon artschool

CRAZY FACES!

Wow! Look at those hairstyles and colors... It's easy to make a face look different – just change the hair! So get out your pencils and felt-tip pens and start changing faces!

HAIR'S HOW...

Copy and color the basic cartoon face shown below, or draw your own. Add some hair – just choose one of the styles from this page.

WHAT HAIR?

Now draw the same face, but add different hair. Keep changing the hairstyle and see how many people you can draw.

HERE'S HOW!

Now try thissss

Now try changing the face shape to suit the hair... or add a moustache and glasses, for a real cartoon disguise.

This hair is tall and spiky! Draw it on a basic face, then try it on a long face, like the one below.

YOO HOO! IT'S ME— CEDRIC!

Draw another basic face. Add ears, a moustache, eyebrows and a smiley mouth. Make the chin square. Add two tufts of hair and a pair of glasses.

SNOOTY FACE
Here's a snooty face. Copy this face on to the shape below.

SNOOTY COPYCAT!
Make sure you exaggerate the eyes and mouth.

SNOOTY FRIEND
Try another snooty face – this time change the hair or add a beard.

Cartoon artschool

A few easy pen strokes make a cartoon face look happy, sad, angry or scared. Changing the shape of the mouth or eyes, can show what a character is thinking or feeling.

A downturned mouth and eyebrows that meet look really mean.

A face with a straight mouth and no eyebrows shows no emotion at all.

Happy, smiling faces have curved mouths and big, round cheeks.

Draw an open mouth with sharp corners and eyebrows in a 'V' to show a tantrum.

A sneaky face can be shown with a small, sideways mouth and eyebrows that meet.

To make a face laugh, give it an open mouth, round cheeks and closed eyes.

A startled face has raised eyebrows, big eyes and a square mouth.

A smug look needs a sideways smile and a half-closed eye.

Dopey or sleepy faces have small, low-down mouths and very droopy eyelids.

HERE'S HOW!

Now try thissss

Cartoons are all about making things look much more extreme than they are in real life. Look at these funny faces.

All the features on these faces are exaggerated: eyes are bulging, mouths are massive, and steam is coming out of the angry man's ears!

HOW'S THIS FOR A FUNNY FACE?

YOU DON'T HAVE TO TRY, CEDRIC.

HORRID FUN!

Try your hand at making truly nasty faces!

First practice a scowl.

Now try a really scary mouth!

Cartoon artschool

DRAWING BODIES FOR THOSE HEADS

Look out... This cartoon head has grown arms, legs and a body! Cartoon people are easy to draw, as they're made up of simple shapes – like rectangles and sausages! Draw the face, then off you go!

To draw your cartoon character you'll need to do some measuring, so the arms, legs and body are the right size. It's easy...

1 First, draw the head and neck. Then, draw a straight, horizontal line underneath.

2 Measure the distance from the top of the head to the line with a ruler. Draw six more lines, across your paper, all the same distance apart.

3 Draw a rectangle for the body over the next three lines down. Add two sausage shapes for each arm and leg, so they take up three lines.

I DON'T NEED SAUSAGES – I'M GORGEOUS AS I AM!

YEAH! A BIG FAT SAUSAGE

HERE'S HOW!

Now try thissss

Now you've drawn your cartoon body, give it hands and feet. Here's how...

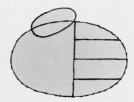

2 Next, draw a small sausage for the thumb and some lines for fingers.

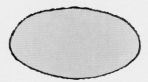

I Feet start out in just the same way as hand, draw a fat, round sausage.

I For the hands, first draw a fat, round sausage for the palm.

3 Finish off the fingers – notice how they're all different lengths.

2 Draw five small sausages for toes. Make the big toe much larger than the rest.

Here's a foot from the front!

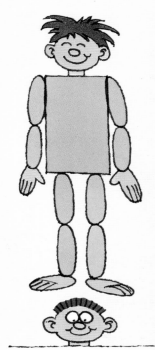

COPY CAT
Copy this cartoon figure in the box below.

WHAT DO YOU MEAN, A BIG FAT SAUSAGE! I'M A NICE SNAKE I AM. BOO-HOO!

ALL THIS TALK OF SAUSAGES HAS MADE ME HUNGRY!

SALT PEPPER

Cartoon artschool

Look out – these characters are off! So take out your pencils and get moving!

WALKING

To make it easy for you to see how he moves, this character has a blue right arm and leg, and a red left arm and leg. As he starts to walk, his right arm and left leg move forward. Next, his right leg and left arm move back. Notice how the legs stay straight.

RUNNING

When this character runs, his arms and legs start to bend. The left leg bends first, then the right leg. When one leg is bent, the other leg is straight. Notice that however fast he runs, this character always has one foot firmly on the ground!

Copy these characters on the right. Then draw some movers of your own! Start with a basic body from with sausage arms and legs. Before you start, take a look at yourself in a full length mirror – move your arms and legs as if you're walking.

Almost all action begins in the same way, so start by drawing a character at a walk and a run. Then copy these jumping and skating characters below.

JUMPING

SKATING

Now try thissss

MOVE IT!
The characters below are on the move! Draw in the next stage – a fast walk and a run!

Cartoon artschool

It's dressing up time! Turn your cartoon characters into dancers, clowns or whoever you like, just by changing their clothes. You can be a cartoon fashion designer!

CLOTHES ON!

Copy this first figure, then dress it up. Start with basic outlines – just follow the shape of the leg for trousers and shorts, or draw a rectangle for a skirt. Then color the clothes and add the details. Look at your own clothes for ideas.

I'M A CLOTHES-FREE AREA, I AM!

MISSING OUTFITS

Wow! This weightlifter is really strong! He has an audience – but they've forgotten their clothes! Draw them each an outfit. Choose from the clothes above, or draw your own.

Dancers, astronauts and waiters need special clothes. Copy their outfits on to the figures below.

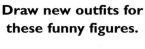

Now try thissss

CHANGE GEAR!
Draw new outfits for these funny figures.

Cartoon artschool

COMMON HOUSEHOLD CARTOON PETS

Look at all these funny creatures! Cartoon animals are easy to draw, as they're made up of simple shapes like circles. Now draw yourself some crazy cartoon pets!

Start with a basic animal shape – draw an oval for the body, circles for the head and ears, a tree-trunk shape for the neck and rectangles for the legs. Then add the feet, tail, eyes and nose.

WADDAYA MEAN, 'SIMPLE'? I CAN BE ANY SHAPE I WANT!!

SNAKES ARE SIMPLE SHAPES.

Now that you've drawn your basic cartoon animal from the side, give it a funny expression. Add a mouth and pupils in the eyes. Make it angry, surprised or happy! To draw an animal from the back or front, instead of the side, start with a circle for the body instead of an oval.

It's easy to draw different types of dogs and cats – just change the shape of the body and legs.

AARGH! A SNAKE!

Look out! That cat looks big and cross! It has a huge, round body and really short legs. wiener dogs have short legs, but long bodies. Don't forget teeth – a few lines in a scowling mouth look fierce, while round teeth in a smiling mouth make a face look friendly!

Now try thissss

FAT CAT!
Copy the angry, red cat above in the space on the right, or create your own cartoon cat.

Cartoon artschool

Create a comical cast of animals! Start with a basic shape, then add lots of details to make your cartoon animal come alive!

★ **Start by copying the simple cartoon dog above. Next, trace your dog, without the eyes, ears and nose. Check out Window Lightbox below for an easy way to do this.**

★ **When you've finished tracing, you're ready to turn your dog into the happy hound on the right! First, draw a long snout, big eyes and a droopy tongue. Then draw sticking-up ears.**

★ **Next, add details – put toes on the paws, add whiskers and draw a collar. Notice how this happy hound has tiny lines all round the edge of his body, so his coat looks hairy. He's even got eyebrows!**

★ **Finally, color your dog – use two shades of brown for the coat, pink for his snout and red for the tongue.**

WINDOW LIGHTBOX

Use your window lightbox to help draw your cartoon animals. Draw your basic cartoon animal. Now, tape your picture on to the glass. Fix a sheet of paper on top. Next, trace your cartoon – without the feature you want to change – like the nose. Remove the paper then draw the new nose.

★ **Here's a curious cat! Again, start by copying the basic cartoon cat on the left, then trace over it, without the details.**

★ **Now the fun starts – make the eyes almond-shaped, and draw an oval snout. Then draw the nose and mouth. Add details to the paws.**

★ **Finally, draw some whiskers, eyelashes and fine lines for fur. Choose any color for your cat – even blue!**

Grrr... tigers on the prowl! Draw your own tiger family – are they happy or sad, or has one tiger eaten too much?! Start with a basic tiger, then add the details.

Draw the basic cartoon tiger at the top, trace over it and copy the details from the tiger on the left. Next, add details from the happy tiger above. Make sure your tiger has big, bold stripes. Notice how the cheeks and inside of the ears are pink.

Look out! This big cat is angry! Give him a scowling mouth and glaring eyes. His friend on the left has eaten far too much! Start with a large, round tummy, then draw the rest.

Cartoon artschool

PAWS, HOOVES, & WINGS: ANIMALS MOVING

Animals move in a totally different way from people. Copy these fun creatures and watch them race off the page! Then try creating more moving animals of your own.

RUNNING LEGS

The way that an animal moves depends on just how fast it is going. Once the pig starts to pick up speed, make sure its feet are drawn high off the ground.

BENDY LEGS

Legs on cartoon animals can bend all over the place, in any way you want. The faster your four-legged friend runs, the more its legs will start stretching out.

LONG LEGS

Ostriches' legs bend the opposite way from ours – their knees face backwards, as their feet go flying forwards. And see how the head and neck change position! This ostrich looks wide eyed and scared!

These animals are having a riotous run around. It's not much of a race when you can't see the finish line! Now try copying them.

Notice how these animals have some different and wonderful expressions. And some of their feet are simply huge!

Cartoon artschool

Have you noticed how some people actually look like animals? Have fun by seeing which animals your friends and family look like!

MAKING FACES
Change the mouth and eyebrows on this man to show anger or surprise.

DOGGY MOODS
Now turn the man into a dog! Draw his ears and add a round nose.

IN THE PINK
For a pig, draw squarer ears. Give him a snout and color him pink!

Someone's taken a tumble! The others don't know whether to laugh or cry. Draw their features to give them different expressions.

Now try thissss

Fill it in!
The characters below all need expressions. They could be happy, sad, worried or even surprised! Use your pencil to draw in their eyes, eyebrows and mouths.

Notice how changing only one feature gives the face a totally different expression!

Cartoon artschool

In cartoon world, even everyday objects can have a life of their own. Find out how to create your own crazy characters!

Tea's up! Bring this teapot to life by turning her spout into a nose and adding eyes with curly lashes! Brew-illiant!

A smooth smile and half-closed eyes make this glass look like a charming guy.

This pink lamp looks sneaky, thanks to his sinister smile and staring eyes. A huge, red hooter adds character, too!

Experiment and find the best place for a face. A wide smile and a bulbous, blue nose breathe life into this spoon, but they wouldn't work anywhere else but the top.

The handle on this happy looking saucepan becomes a long nose when you draw a jolly face around it.

Make the most of an object's shape. Drawing big brows, eyes and a nose above this comb turn its teeth into a bushy moustache!

This friendly flower 'nose' it smells lovely! Its cheerful face and vibrant colors make it a deluxe daisy!

28

HERE'S HOW!

Now try thissss

Bringing objects to life is easy if you do things by the book! Help this hardback with his character and lighten up a candlestick!

1 Draw the outline of a book, making the spine wide enough to fit on features. Add a nose and eyes.

2 Complete the book's face by giving him glasses, a moustache and a smile.

3 Color the cartoon with felt-tip pens, making the features stand out by using different colors.

1 Create a crafty candlestick, adding rings for eyes and a round nose.

2 Dot the eyes and draw a sly smile for a loony light.

3 Paint the candle-stick pale blue, with a darker blue nose. Color the candle cream.

FACE FACTS!
Add a little life to these vases with different funny faces!

Cartoon artschool

Settle behind the steering wheel for a wild, whirlwind tour of cartoon traffic!

What a dopey motor scooter! He only has one big eye, and he doesn't look very bright! Sketch a smiley mouth below his headlight eye and don't forget his lolling tongue!

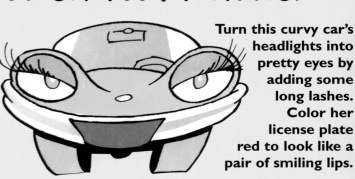

Turn this curvy car's headlights into pretty eyes by adding some long lashes. Color her license plate red to look like a pair of smiling lips.

Sketch a cap above a cheery face to make your cartoon chopper look really chipper!

This motorcycle is raring to go! Draw pupils in his headlights, looking left. Give him a sleek paint job with a tooth pattern and a nose for real personality.

Draw a huge cartoon captain's hat on the roof of this little tugboat. He's very happy chugging along, so sketch a jolly face with a shiny nose on his bow.

Now try thissss

Oh no! We're in trouble! This police car seems angry. Shape the lights on top of the car to look like a hat. Then, add a large, slanted hood over stern, pink eyes and a pair of wing-mirror ears.

MOTOR MOUTHS
Sad, happy or angry? Try filling in the expressions on the three cars below.

This friendly school bus looks more like a teacher as he tootles along! Draw a pair of glasses on his huge windshield, then add a cartoon nose and moustache above a smiling grill.

We have lift off! But, this lazy, bendy rocket isn't racing to get into space. Give him a funny face and add drooping eyelids to show that he's half asleep.

Cartoon artschool

Stop the supervillains! Power up your pencil for some caped, cartoon capers!

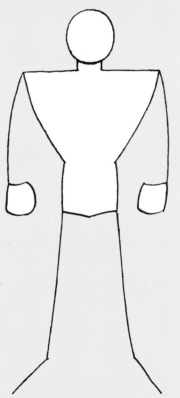 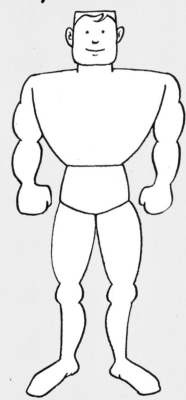 

1 For a superhero shape, start with a triangle for the chest and strong shoulders. Add a head, square hips, legs, and then, arms with two large fists.

2 Next, give your superhero muscles! Draw bumpy lines around each muscle and the knees. Square off the head and add ears, a face and sleek hair.

3 Now, he needs a costume. Draw his boots, gloves, belt, pants and cape. Then, think of a logo – it could reflect his super power – and add it to his outfit.

> I'm Brave Bug! I battle baddies!

> I'm mutant mouse mayhem maker!

> I'm Super Suzy...

> ...I can leap over buildings!

Any creature can be a superhero, but whatever their size, they need a superhero slogan!

Invent incredible powers for your superheroes and villains, then design their dynamic costumes.

Now try thissss

This hunky hero has a stripy suit. Draw his cape flowing out behind him and curved lines to show his arm sweeping around to deliver a mighty, explosive blast. Kapow!

UP, AND AWAY!
Finish off this superhero in flight and color in a costume.

Supervillains have loads of gadgets. Draw an arc covered with small circles for a studded shield. Then, join four arrows to make a grappling hook, attached to this baddie's belt.

sssSay, you can sssSee my sssSkeleton!

X-ray vision is easy. Draw two straight lines coming from the eyes of your supervillain. Then, show the skeleton of whoever he is looking at! ZZZap!

CREATING LIFE IN OUTER SPACE

Create out-of-this-world spaceships, astronauts and little green aliens. Get ready for lift off!

Before you blast into space you'll have to invent a spaceship to travel in. In the crazy world of cartoons, you can make a rocket from just about anything - from dustbins to hot water tanks.

Copy the ideas here or have fun inventing your own spacecraft. But remember, the wackier your invention the better!

IT'S SNAKE-SHAPED!

HERE'S HOW!

Astronauts wear special protective suits. Here's how to suit up your space traveller with style.

1 All astronauts need a helmet, so start off by drawing an oval shape.

2 Next, add a body shape, but make the hands and feet bigger than usual.

Now try thissss

3 Add triangles at the shoulders, give your astronaut gloves instead of hands and add a zipper up the middle of his suit.

4 Add detail to the head – draw a glass cover pulled back to reveal a cheerful space face.

5 Finally, draw in all the detail on the outfit as shown. Now that's space style!

ACE ASTRO
Here's an astronaut we started earlier. Finish it for us by filling in the detail.

Astro boys and girls need tanks of air so they can breathe in space. If you're drawing a spaceman from the side, make sure you draw in oxygen equipment and breathing apparatus.

An easy way to make an astronaut look weightless, as though he is floating in space, is to draw him upside down. Make your picture out of this world by adding in an alien or two!

EASY ALIENS

Aliens are simple to draw. First, sketch in big hands and feet on a small body.

Then, add eyes on stalks.

Hey presto! You're away!

I'M THE FIRST SNAKE IN SPACE

Part 2

RUMBLE!

Bringing it All Together

Cartoon artschool

A cartoon without action is like a party with no ice cream! Use these special effects to make things really move!

In this picture, the runner seems to be floating in mid-air. He doesn't look like he's moving at all.

But, add some movement lines behind him, and it looks like he's dashing straight for the winning line!

In this cartoon, you can't tell if the ball is moving towards the racket or away from it.

Adding curved lines shows which way the racket is moving, and we can see the girl has hit the ball.

Without any special effects, the doctor is just holding the hammer. The patient's leg seems very still.

Now the action comes to life. The doctor whacks the knee with his hammer, and the patient's leg jerks up!

HERE'S HOW!

Explosions are a blast to draw, but you have to be careful – they can look a little messy.

To draw the explosion, start with a circle and a star shape.

Join up the star's points with curved lines. Carefully erase the circle and star shape.

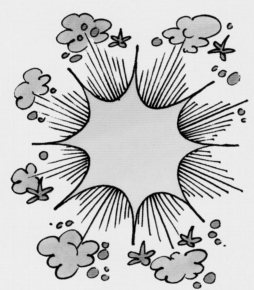

Finish off with puffs of air, extra stars and spiky lines.

Now try thissss

WHAT A BLAST!

Add your own special effects to the balloon and pop can for truly explosive pictures!

Nice return!

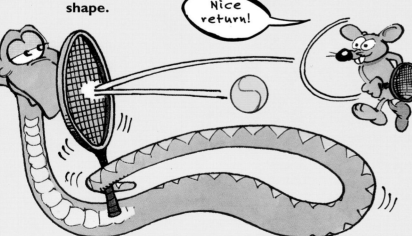

CARTOON COLOR TRICKS

It's time to throw some light on your cartoons. Learn how to make your characters look shady and creepy with clever, color tricks!

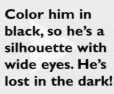

This bald-headed boy looks spooked in the bright light.

Color him in black, so he's a silhouette with wide eyes. He's lost in the dark!

Where you place the lighting in a picture creates a mood. This man already looks pretty mean.

But with a dim light under his chin, he looks really grim! His face has scary shadows where the light doesn't fall – on his forehead and under his evil eyes.

Without special coloring, this girl is just looking to the right.

Add a dark line with pale blue on the left and yellow on the right and she's lit up from the side by a torch or the moon.

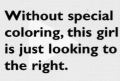
I'm off to practice some more color effects!

ssstrange, I feel like a shadow of my former ssself!

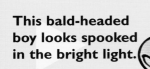

HERE'S HOW!

Now try thissss

Check out some clever ways to use color – and make your characters look off-color!

Brrr! You can tell this girl is freezing by the icy blue color of her skin.

Call a doctor! The green color of this patient tells you he is seriously sick.

What a shocking sight! This kid is so scared, his skin has turned yellow with fright!

Phew! This girl is boiling hot. Her cheeks are bright pink and she's starting to sweat.

IN ACTION!
Color can inject some life into objects, too! Yellow rings set the alarm clock off, and exploding brown liquid makes for a piping hot pot!

FACE PLAY
Use these faces to practice your drawing and coloring skills. Make one face look freezing, one sweltering and another scared.

Cartoon artschool

KEEPING YOUR PERSPECTIVE

Get things into perspective with a few rules. You'll soon be able to show how near, or far in the distance, something is.

Perspective gives an idea of distance. Faraway objects look tiny, but they seem bigger close up. This boy is much shorter than the tree.

But, when the same tree is in the distance, it looks smaller than the boy. The tree hasn't shrunk – the artist has simply drawn it smaller to show how far away it is.

Below, it looks as if the goal posts are small enough for the football player to trip over! They need to look this tiny to show that the goal is a long way in front of him.

When the same player sprints over to the goal posts, he can run under the bar! The posts now look taller than the player because he is standing underneath them.

HERE'S HOW!

These cartoon creatures need to be kept in their place, so start practicing your perspective skills now!

This rhino is a bit too close to the boy for comfort! To show exactly how close, draw the rhino and boy looking eye-to-eye at one another, and keep their feet on the same level.

Whew! To make the rhino keep its distance, draw the horizon line level with the boy's waist. Add the rhino just below the horizon, but much smaller than before.

In this picture, the funny, green bird in the distance looks almost small enough to pick up …

… but as the bird gets closer, it's actually as big as an ostrich! Draw the girl wide-eyed with surprise as the bird towers above her!

Cartoon artschool

Dull scenes can become exciting if you draw them from an unusual angle. Sketch these cartoons for some new views!

Up you go! From this side view, the steep way up doesn't look too tricky for these keen rock climbers.

Yikes! Drawn from above, with the fields below looking tiny, you can see how high up the pair are. Feeling giddy?

I definitely don't have a head for heightsss!

HERE'S HOW!

Tap into the suspense of this tennis match and find the most exciting angle to draw. It's action time!

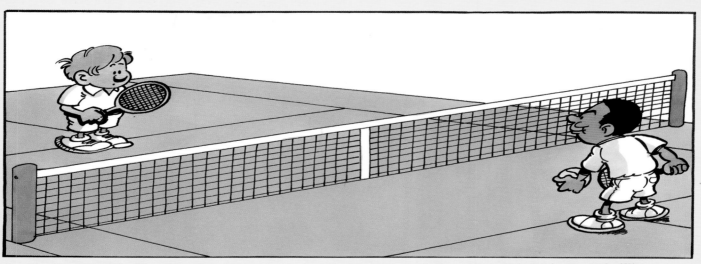

In this first view before play begins, you can see both boys and the net, but it isn't very thrilling.

Add tension by sketching a view from close behind the player with the ball. Now he seems more menacing, and his opponent looks smaller behind the net. This is where things get exciting!

You're a chicken!

No, I'm not! I'm a sssnake!

Cartoon artschool

THE SCENE'S THING

Getting the right setting for your cartoon capers is crucial! Put your characters in their place with these background tips.

Foreground A: This boy has startled eyes, and the girl is looking over her shoulder. They're worried about something behind them, but what is it?

Foreground B: What scares an alien? Without a background you can't tell. His eyes are bulging with fright, so it must be something scary!

Background A: Grrr! This polar bear looks mighty hungry, with his tongue hanging out of his mouth. But what is he chasing across the ice?

Background B: Crash! This alien took a wrong turning at Saturn and has landed with a bump! But, there's no one around to see it!

Cedric's best kept in the background!

HERE'S HOW!

Build up a petrifying, polar bear chase by tracing foreground A and background A from page 4, and then putting them together!

Use a pencil to lightly trace foreground A, with the frightened boy and girl, on to a thin sheet of paper, ready for a background.

Then, trace the icy, Arctic background A, with the running polar bear, on to a second sheet of thin paper.

Lay the foreground tracing over the background and tape them on to a window. Trace the background around the foreground figures.

Now you've got them into trouble! Go over the lines with a black felt-tip pen and then color in your finished picture.

MIX UP

By tracing and combining different foregrounds and backgrounds, you can make your picture tell an exciting new story every time!

IT'S ALL HOW YOU WRITE IT

Make some noise! Find out how to make your cartoons go off with a bang by adding smashing sound effects!

ABCDEFGHIJ KLMNOPQR STUVWXYZ

Practice drawing this chunky cartoon alphabet for some capital effects!

ABCDEFGHIJ KLMNOPQR STUVWXYZ

To make your words leap off the page, add drop shadows. Follow the letter shape and shade a dark shadow slightly below and to the right of each letter.

Mmmmm! Cheese colored paint!

HERE'S HOW!

Now, try shaping and shading your letters to describe different sounds. Write the words around the noisy cartoon action – and don't forget exclamation marks!!!!

CRASH!

These letters are all squashed up as if they've crashed together. Join them with a thick, black outline.

ZOOM! ZOOM!

For something rushing past, write 'Zoom!' Stretch your letters and draw speed lines.

AARGH!

When a character has a clumsy accident, they might shout 'Aargh!' Add crosshatch shading to these letters.

ZAP!

Add 'Zap!' to spells or electrical sparks. Give the letters sharp points and extra outlines.

THUD!

When someone's been knocked down, draw a 'Thud!' Make the letters thick with a chunky drop shadow.

BOOM!

For an explosive sound effect, draw a rounded 'Boom!' with a drop shadow. Color the word in lightening shades.

RUMBLE!

To give sound to an earthshaking tremor, write a 'Rumble!' Short lines around the word add wobble.

KERBAM!

When there's a big crash, write 'Kerbam!' Add crosshatching to the tops and drop shadows. Overlap the letters for a knockout look!

How can I sssleep with all this noise?!

Cartoon artschool

Word up! To give your cartoon characters the gift of gab, you need to master word balloons. Read on to find out how.

A speech balloon's shape can say a lot about the speaker. For a robot's voice, use a rectangular balloon, with capital letters for the words.

> BEEP -- THAT DOES NOT COMPUTE -- BEEP

This girl is so scared, even her speech balloon is shivering! Give it a wobbly border and surround it with short, shaky lines.

> SHUT THAT DOOR!

For an angry, shouting message, give large lettering a spiky-edged balloon. This makes for a voice that's painful on the ears!

> LOOK OUT. IT'S BEHIND YOU!

Most balloons are oval-shaped. Make sure the curved tail from the balloon points towards the mouth of the character who is saying the words.

> THAT'S THE FUNNIEST JOKE I'VE EVER HEARD !!

> It's ssside-splitting!

> I think it's rubbish!

Marilyn is miffed that she doesn't understand the big gag – but she won't admit it! Make her thought bubble cloud-shaped, with a line of little circles leading down to her head.

HERE'S HOW!

There's no need to squeeze your words into speech bubbles if you follow these tips.

Start with the writing. Use a ruler to draw straight pencil lines to write the words in between. Make sure that you leave a space in between the lines.

BEEP -- THAT DOES NOT COMPUTE -- BEEP

When you've written all the words neatly, erase your pencil lines and carefully draw the balloon to fit around the words.

BEEP -- THAT DOES NOT COMPUTE -- BEEP

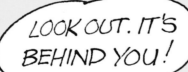

LOOK OUT. IT'S BEHIND YOU!

THAT'S THE FUNNIEST JOKE I'VE EVER HEARD!!

Swap the balloon shapes for these two girls and they look all wrong! Their facial expressions don't match what they're saying.

Now try thissss

BUBBLE TALK

The full force of what Marilyn is saying is lost without speech bubbles! Can you draw the right speech bubbles?

Help! Was that a cat I just spotted?

That Cedric drives me crazy!

Cartoons that don't make sense won't get any giggles. So make sure you set them out clearly for maximum chuckles!

WELL ORDERED

Word balloons should be read from left to right, so think about which of your characters is going to speak first when you plan your scene. Here, the show-off mouthing off is positioned on the left, and the other two boys are responding to his boasting. The boy in the middle is thinking, and the boy on the right is whispering, so his balloon has a broken border.

AIM FOR THE TOP

Try to place your word balloons in the top third of your panels so that they are easy to read and don't spoil the picture. You could draw a light, dotted line as a guide.

LOONY LETTERING

Have fun with different kinds of lettering, like this yell drawn in short, shady lines. Draw the balloon for the screaming sportsman yourself.

GIVE IT A TRY

Now put on your thinking caps and match the words with the balloons in this testing scene. Top marks if you get it right!

YES!! I KNOW IT ALL!

I'LL JUST HAVE A QUICK LOOK!

I DON'T UNDERSTAND A WORD OF IT!

SILENCE!!!

The next time your mom or dad is reading the paper, ask them for the comic page or section. Try rewriting the words while paying attention to where the balloons are and what they look like.

Cartoon artschool

Create your own cartoon strip! Follow a few, simple rules and become an ace, professional cartoonist!

WRITE UP

First, you need to write a funny story that ends with a laugh. Pick a few characters to star in the strip, and keep the plot simple. Give your strip an amusing title.

GET PERSONAL

Next, design your cartoon characters. Decide whether they're going to be funny or glum, sad or bad, and give them names to fit. Sketch them from different angles.

Mr. Green's big, bushy eyebrows, dark-rimmed glasses and turned-down mouth, all add up to a typically stern, teacher look!

This is Charlie. His big feet, freckles and funny ears make him look really playful.

Miles is Charlie's pal. He's laid-back, friendly and loves a good laugh!

What a delightful pair! These seals' bright eyes and big smiles make them look truly cute.

PERFECT PANELS

Now, divide up the main action of your story. Give each scene its own panel. This story is six panels long.

ROUGH AND READY

Draw a rough plan of your strip, arranging the action in your panels. This is called a thumbnail sketch. Start with a panel that sets the scene and introduces your characters. You could include a caption box at the top.

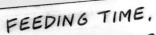

FEEDING TIME.
① TEACHER TAKES PUPILS TO THE ZOO.
② THEY GO TO SEE THE SEALS AT FEEDING TIME.
③ THE SEALS CLAP WITH THEIR FLIPPERS.
④ THE KEEPER THROWS THEM FISH.
⑤ THE TEACHER CLAPS AT THE SEALS.
⑥ A FISH LANDS IN HIS MOUTH TOO!

THUMBNAIL TIPS

★ Make the action in your comic strip move from left to right, as you read it.

★ Leave space in the top third of your panels for word balloons.

★ Draw close-ups of your characters in some panels, then zoom out to show the whole scene in others.

★ The last panel is for the punch line, where the funniest thing happens. It needn't include words – sometimes the picture says it all!

Marilyn is a naturally sssilly ssstoryteller!

Now that the planning is finished, you can draw the page. Follow these panels from pencil to pen to see how it's done!

Use a ruler to draw your panel borders. Sketch your characters in pencil. Use your ruler straight lines to write your lettering on, then draw word balloons with tails pointing to the speakers.

When you've perfected your pencilled artwork, carefully go over the lines with a fine, black felt-tip pen. Then, erase the pencil. Give your characters expressions to suit the scene!

Now, get your colored felt-tip pens out and brightly color your cartoon strip. Make sure your characters have the same colored hair and clothes in all the panels.

GIVE IT A TRY

Finish off this really 'seally' strip with black outlines and bright colors. Then, give yourself a hand!

MR. GREEN TAKES HIS CLASS TO THE ZOO.

NOW, BEHAVE! WE'RE GOING OVER TO LOOK AT THE SEALS!

GREAT! IT'S FEEDING TIME!

ARF! ARF!

CLAP!

CLAP!

ARE YOU HUNGRY? HERE'S A FISH!

WHAT A CLEVER SEAL!

BRILLIANT!

AREN'T THEY CUTE!

CLAP!

CLAP!

HA! HA HA HA!

Try writing your own funny story and make a comic strip using characters you made in the first part of the book.

Cartoon artschool

THINK BIG!

Use this great grid technique to turn teeny, tiny, comic characters into cartoon giants!

I'm so much taller than you, Marilyn!

You're bigger headed, too!

To enlarge a picture, draw a grid of equal-sized squares over it using a pencil and ruler. Lightly draw the same number of squares on to a bigger sheet of paper, making them larger. Now, simply copy what you see in each small square into each large square. To avoid getting yourself confused, number the rows and letter the columns on both grids in the same way. It's easy when you know how!

HERE'S HOW!

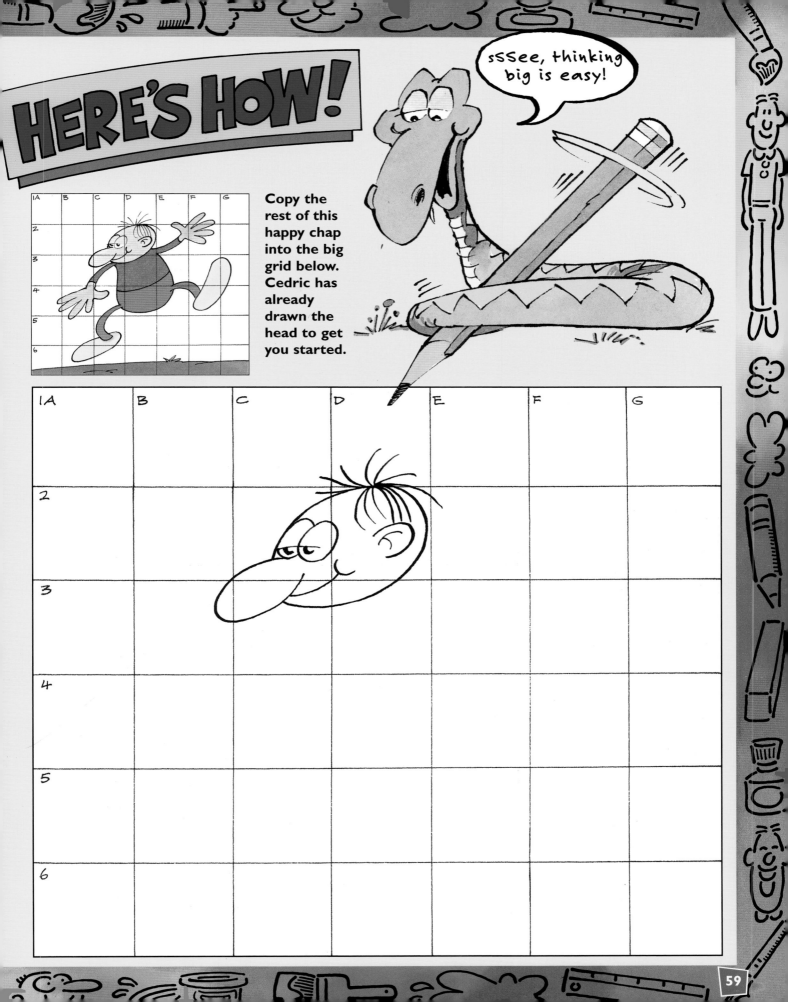

sssee, thinking big is easy!

Copy the rest of this happy chap into the big grid below. Cedric has already drawn the head to get you started.

59

Once you've got the hang of the enlarging technique, you can really hit the big time with some clever tricks! Copy your own pictures or favorite comic cartoons and make them any size you like.

Try zooming in on part of a picture to make it really massive. Just draw four big squares to make this hound's head huge!

It works the other way too! Draw a grid of tiny squares to shrink the terrible terrier down to size!

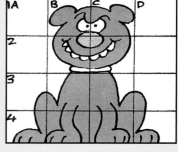

Marilyn thinks Cedric is getting a bit too big for his snake skin! With the help of the grid on the next page, you can give her a bit of a boost, and take Cedric down a peg or two in size!

GIVE IT A TRY

Copy Cedric into the small grid and make Marilyn massive in the tall grid. Their heads have been started to help you.

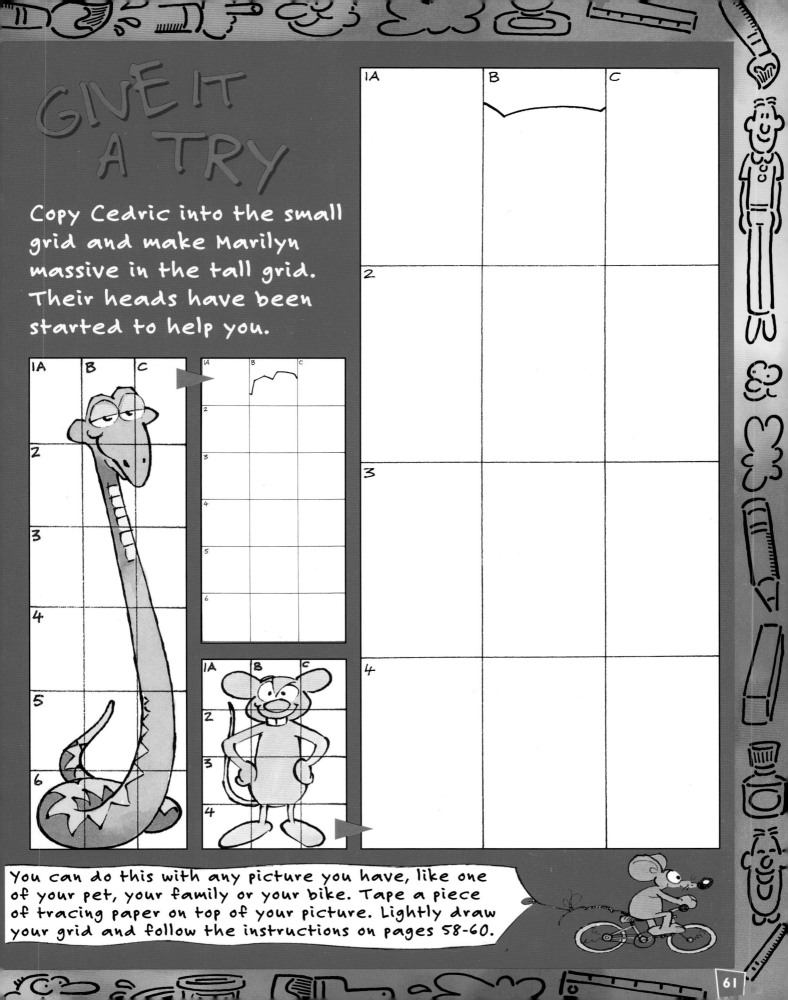

You can do this with any picture you have, like one of your pet, your family or your bike. Tape a piece of tracing paper on top of your picture. Lightly draw your grid and follow the instructions on pages 58-60.

Cartoon artschool

Planning an event or putting on a play? Design your own eye-catching cartoon posters to tell people all about it!

This splashy poster grabs your attention with its bright colors, crazy cartoons and bold lettering. Who could resist going along to see if the Fun Day is as cool as the poster?!

Use jumbo comic lettering for the words on your poster! Cut these out, then play around with them to find the best design that fits on your paper. Glue them down – and your poster is ready to stick up!

Write your messages in zappy borders. This announcement is drawn in a long rectangle with a curvy bottom edge to look like a fairground stall.

Surround your chunky lettering with loud-colored shapes. Try a balloon, a splash or a pointy explosion.

Make the name of your event the largest thing on your poster. Add drop shadows to make the words really stand out.

Crazy cartoons bring the poster to life – the funnier the better!

Check out these lively posters. They have all been designed around a simple, dotted-line grid. Using a grid makes it easy to arrange writing and pictures in blocks or in the center of your sheet of paper.

1 This kickin' design (right) has exciting cartoons to attract the crowds for some action-packed fun.

2 Marilyn and Cedric are the stars of this show (far right), so surround their names with sparkle. Don't forget to put the date, time and place on your poster.

3 This poster (right) has dash! The speedy picture of Cedric and Marilyn, and RUN in very large letters, let you know instantly what it's all about!

4 Musical notes and wacky, wobbly writing really make this festival (far right) festive! Check out those back-to-front Fs, too.